PANDEMIC ALMANAC

Also by Rachel Hadas

POETRY
- *Love and Dread*
- *Poems for Camilla*
- *Questions in the Vestibule*
- *The Golden Road*
- *The Ache of Appetite*
- *The River of Forgetfulness*
- *Laws*
- *Indelible*
- *Halfway Down the Hall*
- *The Empty Bed*
- *Mirrors of Astonishment*
- *Pass It On*
- *A Son from Sleep*
- *Slow Transparency*
- *Starting from Troy*

PROSE
- *Piece by Piece*
- *Talking to the Dead*
- *Strange Relation*
- *Classics*
- *Merrill, Cavafy, Poems, and Dreams*
- *The Double Legacy*
- *Living in Time*
- *Form, Cycle, Infinity: Landscape Imagery in the Poetry of Robert Frost and George Seferis*

TRANSLATIONS
- *Dionysiaca of Nonnus*, Book 16
- *The Iphigenia Plays of Euripides*
- *The Helen of Euripides*
- *The Oedipus of Seneca*
- *Other Worlds Than This*

EDITED ANTHOLOGIES
- *The Waiting Room Reader II*
- *The Greek Poets: From Homer to the Present* (coeditors Peter Constantine, Edmund Keeley, and Karen Van Dyck)
- *Unending Dialogue: Voices from an AIDS Poetry Workshop*

PANDEMIC ALMANAC

RACHEL HADAS

RAGGED SKY PRESS
PRINCETON, NEW JERSEY

Copyright © 2022 by Rachel Hadas
All rights reserved

Published by Ragged Sky Press
270 Griggs Drive, Princeton, NJ 08540
www.raggedsky.com

Library of Congress Control Number: 2021950391
ISBN: 978-1-933974-45-3

Design: Jean Foos and Dirk Rowntree
Author photo and cover art: Shalom Gorewitz

Printed in the United States of America

First Edition

Contents

February 29, 2020 | 3

Ides of March MMXX | 5

A Universe of Dread | 6

Fusion and Diffusion | 7

Mud Season | 9

Inner and Outer Weather | 11

Pinecones | 12

Everything and Nothing | 14

But Who Is Counting | 15

Sourdough Starter | 16

The Seeds | 17

Trying to Get to School | 20

Little Free Library, Turners Falls | 22

Shopping Upstairs | 24

Bouncing Bet | 27

Zoom and Zoom | 29

Do You Believe in Ghosts? | 31

Mysterious Microclimates | 33

That Patch of Warmth | 34

The Labyrinth, the Septic Tank | 35

Labyrinth, Unfinished | 36

Halloween 2020 | 38

Harvest and Tide | 39

Patience and Fortitude | 41

Still | 43

In the Cloud | 44

Preexisting Conditions | 46

Blursday out of Breughel | 48

Grief Seminar | 51

The Cave | 53
The Ramparts | 55
In the Cold Courtyard | 57
The Second Shot | 58
The Cave Again | 59
Tarot in Straus Park | 60
Too Soon to Tell | 62

Afterword | 65
Acknowledgments | 67
About the Author | 69

PANDEMIC ALMANAC

February 29, 2020

New York, February 2020

As if we knew but didn't know we knew.
February 29: Leap Day,
an extra day, an ordinary day,
predictable even in being extraordinary—
a bonus day in the old dispensation
we couldn't guess was close to termination.
When did we start to sense the great subtraction?

Leap Day, then. And I was on my way
to catch a train to go to Tarrytown
(people still had a schedule and a plan,
mapping the hours to their destination)
to run a four-hour class on poetry—
specifically, tailored to the day,
on poems that performed a lyric leap:
the way the mind hopscotches, A to C
or D or Z, a little lateral hop
or skip, a sudden swerve, a syncopation.

I waited for the train. Grand Central Station:
tourists and travelers in circulation,
all of them aimed at some desired location,
throngs chatting, texting, pausing to gaze up
at the iconic ceiling's constellations.
A pregnant woman in a scarlet coat
posed for a photo with a selfie stick.
Her baby must be six weeks old by now.
Waiting for my train, could I foresee
crowds would soon be prohibited by law?
Could anyone imagine the great hall
would within weeks be scoured clean of all
humanity? Just dust motes in the sun.
Idle tracks. An empty waiting room.
Whoever sensed it didn't want to see.

That extra day, that ordinary day,
I got where I was going on the train
and taught the lyric leap, as per the plan;
then, tired, happy, bathed in poetry,
caught a train and travelled back again,
retraced my steps. Grand Central one more time.
Maybe make that Grand Central one last time.

Looking back now, I can see I saw,
that Leap Day when we leaped with poetry,
the cold blue morning light, the dappled sky,
the river silver grey as we rode by.
But what no one was prepared to see:
not quite a harbinger, since it was there
already. No, a searchlight raked the air
invisibly, masked by morning's glare.
That searchlight still is circling everywhere,
and everyone's a target—you and me.
And yet with the bewilderment and fear,
upheaval on a scale we scarcely see
even though we sense it in the air,
companion to our stunned anxiety,
something else persists invisibly,
something that isn't going anywhere,
something that is still here.

Ides of March MMXX

New York, March 2020

Nothing new,
but it feels like an end.
An end that's new.
This end is now?
No, I said new.
But who
could hear me through my mask?
Don't ask.
Love
wears a glove.
I want to touch my friend.

This fear feels new.
We've all forgotten how
to live with it, to live it
day by day. And each
day begins anew,
begins a new
now we do not know,
oh no,
do not yet know.

A Universe of Dread

New York, March 2020

Pandemic world where nothing's as it seems:
we wake up to a universe of dread.
The economic palimpsest of dreams

yields to an incessant spate of screens.
Caught between the living and the dead
(pandemic world where nothing's as it seems),

we are told to shelter in our homes.
Pull the covers up over your head.
The hardwired virology of dreams

dictates we want to know what all this means.
Where is that cave where the sick bats first bred?
Pandemic globe where nothing's as it seems:

each morning we awaken to fresh memes.
The schematized corona's knobby; red.
Pandemic world where nothing's as it seems
except the slippery palimpsest of dreams.

Fusion and Diffusion

New York, March 2020

You and I
were at Book Culture, hoping
to sell a couple of books,
as we had often done before. Before.
No luck,

so we ventured further down the block.
Morningside Heights turned into Herald Square.
Here was another store, a bigger store
which had two stories. I went up the stairs.
You waited down below.

But on the second floor
what was displayed was no longer books
but boots and shoes—footwear
I knew no one would need or want to buy.
Not now. Maybe never.

The only shopper in the place was me.
I wanted to get out
and find you on the street
where you would be waiting,
patient as ever, gentle, sweet,

my love, my anchor
in a sea of terror.
Both unsold books I clutched were by my father.
Old Wine, New Bottles;
Hellenistic Culture: Fusion and Diffusion

still tucked under my arm,
I walked back down the stairs.
And yes, I know,
all of us now know,
our vision is pitifully incomplete.

But I know too—I knew—
I looked for you;
I called and called you, but you weren't there.
Fusion and diffusion.
No one was there.

Mud Season

Vermont, April 2020

So. We've made our way up here
and things look pretty good so far.
They didn't stop us at the border—
no policemen to keep order,
poised to pounce on an out-of-state
and less than welcome license plate.
We venture out. The air feels clear.
The chief contagion up here: fear.
Here comes someone. Adjust your mask.
A friend? A stranger? Do not ask.
The fear's ubiquitous and stark:
what can I catch from a tree's bark?
Or if I bend down to pick
up a pinecone or a stick,
what's my chance of getting sick?
Is it dangerous to touch
a maple or brush by a birch?
How long does the virus linger
on a package or a finger?
Must we swab groceries, clothes, shoes, mail?
Anxiety's out of control.
Shrinking from one another, we
leave room for more anxiety—
"we" being not, love, you and me,
but citizens of this state and town
who do their part by hunkering down,
their brand of social isolation
honed by years of habituation.
They hunker down and then glance out.
Wait. What was all the dread about
that cast a pall on everything?
Change is coming. Remember spring,
sweet and green and wet and warm?
Something is near that will transform

this end-of-winter's chilly blast
and relegate it to the past.
Let's take a walk. Put on your mask.
But even through it take a breath
and inhale pollen instead of death.
A bird sings on a branch—still bare,
but change is waiting in the air.
Instead of thinking about disease
let's walk among the leafless trees.
Believe in seasons. Trust in time.
Spring and renewal always rhyme,
and rhyming is no accident.
We'll wonder soon where winter went.
Today: blue sky. Mud. Melting snow.
Where did all the terror go?
Tomorrow: snow squall, mud, and sun.
Gingerly we begin again.

Inner and Outer Weather

Vermont, April 2020

Sun sleet snow-squalls rain hail sun again:
all day long we kept on changing our clothes
to keep up with the changes in the weather.
Each episode was slivered into such fleeting wisps
that in between the chill from a door left open
and wet wood hissing in the smoky stove,
cloud shadows and the kindness of the air
kept changing. Just so with inner weather:
these constant waves of gratitude and fear,
pounding, receding, can only be predicted
as April in Vermont can be predicted:
sleet, hail, snow, sun, and every now and then
a rainbow gleaming like a tearful smile.

Button up your sweater. Put your coat on.
Don't forget your mittens or your hat:
Our mothers' voices back when we were children,
our own voices when our kids were young.
Don't get your feet wet.
Stay warm. Be careful.
We are all children now.
Put on your mask.

Pinecones

Vermont, April 2020

Absolute not knowing
and knowing we do not know.

Halfway up the hill,
behind still-leafless trees, something is hiding.
If my granddaughter were here,
she and I would scour this path for pinecones
and tuck each nugget, each synecdoche,
into our baskets.

Alone I gather pinecones.
Back home, I toss a few into the fire.
After seventy lucky years,
it is so easy to forget the rough
patches in one's own story,
let alone how life has been forever:
war, starvation, plague,
suffering, burnt-out hopes, more suffering.

We forget, until uninvited knowledge
visits: not recollection but fear.

I meant to gather fears
and bring them home and toss them into the fire.
But climbing this cold hill
in the hush before the whenever arrival of spring,
barely a breath of wind in the pines
and the few birds left waiting,

silent, suspended,
uncertain what I thought to find or lose,

I look for fear. It is nowhere to be seen.
Is it hiding behind that slim young tree?
Was it ever there?

Even if it has left, will it return
and pounce and strike and mock,
wave its pale banner, float away again?

Absolute not knowing
and knowing we do not know.

Everything and Nothing

Vermont, May 2020

Everything I need is already here.
This decades-old *Smithsonian* magazine
a neighbor gave me makes it all too clear

I hadn't known that I was looking for
an article on Robert Louis Stevenson.
Was everything I needed really here?

How long has it been now—a month? No, more.
And when did we emerge from quarantine?
Simple questions; answers never clear.

Each dawn aims its glaring scarlet spear
as morning takes a breath and starts again.
Count: our remaining time begins right here.

Turn the page. The Stoic calendar
offers sober lessons we can learn.
Irrelevant? If only. Urgent; clear.

This interlude feels now cramped, harsh, austere,
and now capacious as an ocean.
Everything and nothing: both are here,
precariously balancing on fear.

But Who Is Counting

Vermont, June 2020

I have been studying how I may compare
our matching morning dreams
which of us woke up wanting to weep
but look the dawn in russet mantle clad
though this is more blood-red
three months but who is counting
dig deeper into patience
there is nothing but time
questions and silences
green realm edged with nightmare
and rise and face the day
house with a different view from every window
news from every quadrant of the sky
but who is counting

Sourdough Starter

Vermont, June 2020

To punch what happened down and keep it down
ought to be a simple chore. Yet still,
resilient, the dough swells up to fill
above the brim that bowl there in the sun.
One batch of sourdough starter, it is said,
can trace its lineage generations back.
Each fresh loaf carries on the tangy smack,
fermented yeastiness, inherited,
revised, enhanced by its long passage through
decades of kneading by uncounted hands.
Let rise; bake; eat. Leftover starter's fed
with flour and water. And the sour dough
rises again, again meets the demands
the living keep on making: *Give us bread.*
And starts again. It's living. It's not dead.

The Seeds

Vermont, June 2020

to Sara Grossman

My former student sent me six or seven
little homemade packets—folded paper
labelled and taped. Inside each packet
she'd tucked a few heritage seeds:
squash, lettuce, kale, peas, more I am forgetting.

April in Vermont. Not a warm April.
Still way too cold to plant the seeds outside.
I took dirt from the not-yet-tilled garden
and planted the seeds in an empty egg carton
and labelled each oval hollow
and set the egg box on a sunny sill.
May. Snow again. The weather
mercurial as our feelings day by day:
Sun, snow, late April,
Snow, sun, early May.
The world pure white; and then the morning melt.

Eventually the seeds began to sprout.
but the cats, noticing this, climbed one night
onto the sill and nibbled the young shoots,
tender and green and irresistible.
Or could it have been mice?
I moved the egg box to a higher place.
And by the second week (was it?) in May
the ground was ready, and the sun was warm.
The seeds were ready. I was ready. So
I planted the little shoots,
gnawed as they were—they never had stopped growing.
But by this time the labels
had gotten wet and blurred or fallen off.
The one thing I was sure of was the pea plants.

Fast forward (though it feels both fast and slow
in this timeless time):
the second week of June.
The peas—two plants—are burgeoning,
green tendrils curling, reaching
for something to cling to and then to climb on.
And nestled next to them a mysterious bonus:
a hardy squash plant. I was going to move it
but squash and pea looked so happily intertwined,
flourishing cheek by jowl, I let them be.

What is the most beautiful thing
on the black earth? asked Sappho.
I say it is what one loves.

The beautiful pea plants hopefully pushing upward
out of the black earth
obey their nature despite the pandemic.
Despite the pandemic, spring is in the air.
The garden doesn't care.
The virus, also obedient to its nature,
follows its own laws.

Sara, thank you for sending me these seeds,
for thinking to do it and then doing it.
Even if most of them got lost
(my heedlessness) in their passage to the earth,
one or two have survived. I can see them growing.
Sara, student, poet, teacher,
lover and scholar of nature, brown fields, green fields,
lover of ruined cities and of gardens,
in sending these seeds you gave me
an unexpected gift, a perfect gift
for this place and time.
The seeds, a gift of hope, also signify
your impulse to show your gratitude
for what I barely remember having given you,
because in giving whatever it was I gave you
I too was obedient to laws

I was barely aware of,
laws inscribed in you, in me,
in this young pea plant sending out its tender shoots,
ready to reach, connect, cling, climb, and hold,
and spread, and grow.

Trying to Get to School

Vermont, June 2020

Dream: halfway to my destination
I remembered something I'd forgotten
and turned around so I could get
it back before it was too late.

But making my way from A to B
could not be managed easily.
Locked courtyard, blocked alleys, a high wall—
I had to cross or climb them all.

I tried and tried without success.
Wherever I turned: NO ACCESS,
no way to reach the subway station
and get from there to my destination

across the river and into a room
I'd open the door to (what was Zoom?),
enter, talk, listen, and engage
with my students, forgetting age,

and tell them, before time ran out,
what reading and writing were about.
Gathered together in one place,
to talk and listen, face to face:

this, my dream was telling me,
was something that could no longer be.
Henceforth it wouldn't be allowed
to be part of any crowd.

Locked courtyards and blocked alleyways,
our isolated nights and days,
no hands held up or questions asked,
the eager faces muffled, masked,

all siloed in our separate spaces,
and interposed between us: stasis.
I knew already there was no
way to get where I had to go.

The dream I dreamed six months ago:
prophetic, but no longer true.
Now crowds have gathered—still masked, yes,
but shouting against voicelessness.

The streets are full, the atmosphere
ardent, insistent. Where is fear?
Forgotten in the hope and flow.
Justice is contagious too.

Little Free Library, Turners Falls

Vermont, June 2020

Having gone out of our way
to get to a dispensary,
we happened on this library,
its modest random contents free
to anyone who happened by.
Except there was no one but me
and my husband. Empty street,
brick sidewalks and a bench to sit—
the tiny Massachusetts town
swathed and shuttered in lockdown
except this little library box,
which had no need of any locks.
I peered inside. What was the book
I serendipitously took?
The title stopped me: *Crones Don't Whine.*
So if you do whine, does that mean
you fail to qualify as crone?
Are crones what we aspire to be?
Women do age variously,
but we all age. You may not whine,
but no one is exempt from time.
The years take individual tolls,
shrink or expand our separate souls.
Sometimes an aging woman's face
crusts into a carapace,
stiff, lapidary, leathery
landscape of time's geography.
Whining is something not to do.
But can't tears be allowed to flow?
Tears, blood, lymph—all irrigate.
We need this moisture early, late
in life. Crones do not whine: agreed.
But pain's a constant, and the need
to let it out, give it a name

shouldn't be a source of shame.
It's just a sign of being human,
whether you are a man or woman.
This need never diminishes.
The book was cradled on my knees
as we drove home through leafy green
into the strange embrace of June
and open-ended quarantine.
I didn't feel the need to whine.
I'm practicing to be a crone.

Shopping Upstairs

Vermont, June 2020

for my grandfather, Lewis Parke Chamberlayne
*so-called periods of transition (if all periods are not so)—
those centuries when a new religious or political system
is growing up amidst the decay of the old one.* —LPC

Since the contagion isn't stopping,
upstairs is where I do my shopping—
upstairs, the attic of the mind
where childish things are left behind
for us to uncover or rediscover,
unearthing treasures over and over,
pawing through time like an eager lover.
Past years add up: a palimpsest,
a drift of papers, an old desk,
yellowing folders from which school...
reuse, recycle, or retool.
Upstairs is ancient history.
Back at ground level, what do I see
in every day's kaleidoscope?
Terror, stasis, glints of hope.
Ghosts of evils that came before,
plague and depression, civil war,
take on new life. So here we are.
Repurposed T-shirts make a quilt.
Each day's fresh headlines spell out guilt.
Zombies pop up with renewed
appetite, and seek warm food.
As if just roused from hibernation,
they shamble toward our—vacation?
Maybe. Weeks back, a snowy spring.
Today, zucchini blossoming,
raspberries plumping, peas in flower,
the gardens growing by the hour.
Late June: summer in its glory.

But this is hardly the whole story.
The past is where I do my shopping;
the present moment's stalled and stopping.
The season hums with green and growth,
true; but not the only truth.
History's coming home to roost.
My grandfather sends a post—
essays that made their way to me
through complex serendipity,
not papers someone tucked away
but messages received today.
These meditations on my screen
from 1911, 12, 13,
taken to heart as soon as seen....
More than a century since he died.
Did he write these for me to read?
Who are writers speaking to?
Unknown descendants—is that who?
A Virginian through and through,
and son of an artillery
captain who fought under Lee
(a name now in the news each day),
my grandfather on my screen
is pondering transition.
Words aren't statues. They don't fall,
as Lee has, from his pedestal.
Word aren't statues. Let them stay.
Don't delete what they have to say.
He sensed the pattern—something new
growing from the old's decay.
But wasn't every era, though,
transitional? He wondered, who,
born in 1879,
died in 1917
at thirty-eight. And here I am,
in late June, 2020,
grandchild he never lived to see,
much older than he lived to be.

He left these essays I digest.
I do my shopping in the past.
If you have the time and patience,
the past yields food for ruminations.
The future? Hard to think about
until this virus peters out,
which it shows no sign of doing.
The garden's parched. The lawn needs mowing.
Sheltering in place in this green space
where summer shows its shining face,
we're teetering between two ages
as the pandemic rages, rages.

Bouncing Bet

Vermont, July 2020

On a dirt road long ago,
frothy pink and white flowers grew.
My mother called them Bouncing Bet.
A French-Canadian family,
five or six children, named Bessette,
lived in a house across the way.
Celeste, the eldest, played with me.

Our family took a stroll one day,
the height of summer, late July,
down the road toward the Bessettes,
who kept (it's coming back to me)
pigs in a pen—two pigs or three.

I tossed a watermelon rind
into the pen and took a step
too close. One big pig grunted, then
tried to bite my sneakered toe.

The guests who walked with us that day
were F. D. Reeve and Helen, his wife.
One pig peed. "He's making pee,"
said Alya Reeve, then maybe five
(a therapist now in Santa Fe).

Frank and Helen Reeve divorced
years later, and my father died,
later my mother. The Bessette brood
moved out. The Klosses and their small
family moved in; left. Last of all
Peggy and Terry Larney came
with Katie and Jackie and their dog
Molly. The parents live there still.
One daughter's living down the hill,
the other one not far away.

Molly has long gone off to play
in the hunting grounds in the sky.

And now again it is July.
The Bouncing Bet's in bloom today.
We saw the lilacs bloom in May—
we came up earlier this spring
and will stay later into fall
now that the pandemic's come,
draping the country with its pall,
darkening the world. Still, everywhere
flowers are blooming in the sun.
Bees in the bee balm buzz and hum.
I was reminded by my dream
(Bouncing Bet in a rose-pink dawn):
these flowers will be here when we're gone.

The things we know but do not say,
so that we forget we know,
so that we know and do not know—
things we ignore from day to day
until a waft of fragrance, hum
and low-tech zoom of bumblebee
and ruffled flowers, pink and white
(who are you now, Celeste Bessette?
Somebody's grandmother, I bet)
warn us: Remember. Get it right.
We will be here. You will not.

Zoom and Zoom

Vermont, July 2020

Thank you, pandemic. I had stood
and dithered at an open door
you waved me through, so I am here.
Goodbye to classrooms—yes, for good.

Classrooms of flesh and blood, I mean,
persons, bodies—these are gone.
And if and when they do return
I will long have left the scene.

Spending a reluctant hour
in an online webinar
(redundant phrase) has made it clear:
a bell is tolling *Nevermore*.

The overwhelming takeaway
from that session had to do
with dialects, the old and new:
what we can and cannot say.

Verbs like "understand" and "know"—
avoid them. What they signify
is difficult to quantify.
Better to use "describe" or "show"

to specify the outcome we
desire. The students must attest
their competencies test by test.
Meanwhile they are assessing me.

Outcome. Assessment. Canvas. Zoom.
So many points for this or that.
Give them a prompt. Or let them chat.
Five minutes in a breakout room.

But I am breaking out of there:
I leave the meeting, blank the screen,
that tiny smudgy windowpane,
and flee the confines of my square.

Late this August afternoon,
late in my life, I've made the choice
to de-digitize my voice,
exit the virtual meeting room,

and pivot (verb one constantly
sees in these days of swerve and slide),
and walk away and sit outside
and sense the season passing by

and note the shadows on the lawn
and listen to the hummingbirds—
wings, beaks, vibrations, no words—
zoom in and out of the bee balm.

Do You Believe in Ghosts?

Vermont, August 2020

for Bryanna Tidmarsh

Do you believe in ghosts? she asked.
New world of specters, muffled, masked:
now is the moment for this query,
when every encounter's eerie
and we can only recognize
familiar faces by their eyes.
Not quite certain who we see
and navigating cautiously,
we make our slow and blurry way
through the labyrinth of each day.
If human faces are concealed
by mask or shield or mask and shield,
much else is suddenly crystal clear—
not that it wasn't always here,
but habit blithely papered over
structures we now must rediscover.
The virus casts a lurid glow
on what we knew and didn't know,
leaving us with no excuse
to ignore forces on the loose.
In crowded streets, we seem to sense
history's weighty consequence,
not dead, and therefore not a ghost—
the past is never even past.
Still, I believe in ghosts, in all
the clouds of the invisible
that now beset us: memory,
injustice, virus, ancestry,
the gifts and poisons of each spirit
that we unknowingly inherit,
the countless energies that fly
unnoticed by the human eye.
So much, so much we cannot see!

That is what *ghost* means to me.
Pandora opened up her jar;
out flew the evils, fast and far,
famine and pestilence and war.
Hope, last, remained inside somehow—
hope that sustains us here and now,
poised, our most beloved ghost,
between the future and the past.

Mysterious Microclimates

Vermont, August 2020

In the middle of the morning the dream came back.
Curled in the crook of my arm,
a tiny child whom I was teaching to speak
repeated the words I said,
which may have been *stopwatch guilty dandelion
epic*—all words of more than one syllable,
carefully repeated, now all gone,
dissolved into the morning.

Julia Zooms on the porch.
Someone's mask discarded on the table.
A thunderstorm roils and rumbles, willful squalls
recalling the apocalyptic poems
I have been struggling to read
on a pale printout.
The drought persists.

To walk between the trees and suddenly sense,
like bands of warmer or cooler
water when one is swimming,
mysterious microclimates,
zones of inscrutability—
moods work like that:
a patch of air, a gust from where, one weather
bleeds into another.
The humidity of the inescapably human.

Leave the screen, get up, and go outside.
Stones need shifting in the labyrinth.
Something gleams in the branches;
light livid, but no rain.
Julia Zooms on the porch.
The dough is rising.
In the middle of the morning, the dream came back.

That Patch of Warmth

Vermont, August 2020

August. Midday. Look up: flawless sky
until a cloud sprouts; sidles; suddenly
blots out the sun. Wind troubles the trees;
stops. A hush. A stillness. Ominous?
Not really. It will start again, and soon.
Stopping these alternations can't be done.
Incessant changes won't be kept at bay.
Why didst thou promise such a beauteous day?
complained the Bard, who was expecting no
reply. I'll go in now and check the dough
rising gently in its yellow bowl
on the kitchen table in a pool
of sunlight for which the two cats compete.
That patch of warmth has shifted as I write.

The Labyrinth, the Septic Tank

Vermont, August 2020

Blue and gold day. Sharp clear sky.
Late August: time is racing by.
Long dark shadow-fingers loom
so early now each afternoon
that I am torn: should I lie down
in your arms in our dim bedroom
and miss a precious hour of sun
when it is also wholly true
that I long to lie with you
and spend an hour—more—in the mesh
of arms and legs, mouths, breath, and flesh?
Still, if I choose to raise my head
from the activities in bed
and look out at the cedar tree,
light slants. Time's moving visibly.

Red sunset. Misty morning sky.
The rhythm of the everyday.
The septic tank, the labyrinth—
both new and both as old as myth:
variations in the groove
habit and terror, work and love
have worn in us. Take last week's trench—
first locate a sewage stench
(we walked for decades on old shit
but till now barely noticed it),
then excavate and then replace,
fill up the hole and plant new grass.
Replacement happens for a reason.
Time passes. All things have their season.
Red alert: two dead leaves fall.
The pandemic drapes its pall.

Labyrinth, Unfinished

Vermont, October 2020

At the lip of the still-in-progress labyrinth,
I sit down on a stump
and run my fingers through the moss
mantling the bark like soft green hair.

The sun is rising, and a caul of dawn
wraps the flank of Pumpkin Hill and blurs
the past how many months? We've all lost count.
April; summer; suddenly October,

calendar out of focus, wavering timeline
one wants and also hesitates to map,
record and memorize and not forget,
or else obliterate.

The labyrinth, abetted by the drought,
translates visions into dusty brown
demotic. Pinecone, pebble, leaf, or stick:
which, my mind elsewhere, did I stumble on?

Time and nature lack specific weight.
Months flicker. Hours sag.
A leaf is heavy and a stone is light.
I pace around the labyrinth; sit again.

If I sit long enough, if I am silent,
voices from the past and future float
toward me, trailing wisps of prophecy
and memory. Shadows, sharper by the day,

point toward an end and a beginning.
Can you capture time
as it ghosts through golden trees?
Labyrinth, unfinished, offering

your challenge and your refuge, your technique
of winding inward and then out again,
change and endurance spiraling with hope,
Let me in again and I will walk.

Halloween 2020

Vermont, October 2020

10:30 in the morning.
In the Defiant stove,
the fire breathes behind me.
I sit and face the sun.
The cats, heat-seeking missiles,
occupy the warm oblong
on the tablecloth from Kumasi.
The garden through the window:
drowned in fallen leaves.
Foxy Epoxy,
our foot-high statuette,
looks chilly as the fountain
nymph outside the Plaza—
slim ladies lightly draped
or wholly in the nude,
comfortable in summer
but too exposed for fall
now sliding toward winter.
Will I see the Plaza again?
When we return to the city,
if we return to the city,
will the city be the same?
Questions; no answers.
I thought nothing was moving:
dewdrops on the woodpile,
jewels of hanging light.
Nothing moving? Sun
shifts and the cats shift with it.
Across the bright striped fabric
dark shadows stretch already.
When did this begin?
Questions. No answers.
The only moment now.

Harvest and Tide

Vermont, November 2020

for Molly Peacock

Sit still an hour if you can.
Receive the harvest coming in,
baskets of bounty. Did I dream
that minuscule Athenian
apartment? Or Jerusalem:
wedged outside the Airbnb
in the German Colony,
that sliver of a balcony,
where, cramped beside my love, I sat.
We watched the moon rise, heard a cat
courting or fighting—a shrill scream.
As memory can recede to dream,
so dream can morph to memory.
A figment? A reality?
How can I tell? And do I care?
In this space/time where nothing's near,
nothing, also, is all that far.
Flotsam and jetsam drift toward shore,
borne on the tides of webinar.
Who would have thought that Cicero
would be discussed on Zoom? With no
warning, once more my father and I
(it all comes back) make our slow way
right through *De Senectute,*
sentence by sentence, page by page,
adolescence next to age.
Parsing a period clause by clause,
I absorbed all kinds of laws.
And every scrap retrieved replays
through these brief November days—
days uneventful? Yes and no.
Some days all but overflow.
Some days are vessels that contain

the stored-up contents of my brain,
distilled from all I ever learned.
Life went on. The pages turned.
The long hiatus now affords
silence and space: I hear the words.
I'm trudging out to the woodshed;
rhythms resound inside my head.
I climb the hill; soliloquies
declaim behind the naked trees.
Poems I didn't know I knew
chime faithfully as an echo.

Harvest, you called it. I said tide;
whichever, gifts from far and wide
bestowed on you, dear friend, and me.
Poetry's generosity
and durability accrue
to us—we're lucky, me and you.
Not only us. Linked poets stand
across the landscape, hand in hand.
One hand is writing; one extends
out to the circle of poet friends,
a gyre that widens. Listen. Wait.
The bounty will accumulate.

Patience and Fortitude

Vermont, November 2020

Shadows by eleven—ten—in the morning
stretch long fingers across the table. Lolling
cats, two plump striped heat-seeking missiles, bask there.
        Hours of daylight

slant and dwindle. Noon? Afternoon already.
Shafts of light brush everything with russet:
dead stalks, woodpile, the two red squirrels that frisk there.
        Leaves, wet and gleaming,

camouflage the two terra-cotta lions,
also russet, crouching, a pair of sphinxes,
on either side of the steps leading to the garden,
        guarding the threshold—

liminal, but portal to what transition?
Halloween, Election Day, a birthday,
orange dawns, and daylight snuffed out so early...
        Fortitude. Patience.

Each new day is asking us to dig deeper
into whatever meager store of these virtues
might still be available. Every night brings
        visions of danger:

corridors and tunnels and streets and classrooms,
unmasked mobs, encounters and fights and longings
cradled, nurtured, buried, lamented. Morning:
        where did the dream go?

Numberless months: where did they disappear to?
Where did the sun go, vanishing so early?
This pandemic, when will it end? Or will it?
        We ask like children.

We are children; powerless. Also aging,
weighed down, burdened by—can we even, slogging
through this darkness visible, call it knowledge?
                One thing I have learned:

since it has become a constant companion,
breathing presence to which we are now accustomed,
walking with us, sharing our long black shadows,
                fear can befriend us.

Still

Vermont, November 2020

Still. As in motionless
or silent, brimming with expectation.
As in affirmative with qualification:
still; nevertheless.

At or up to the time indicated.
Are you still here?
The days are getting shorter. Winter's near.
Possibly we've just procrastinated,

put off the inevitable. Still...
the thought, the sentence trail off like a sigh.
Seven months have gone by.
We came in early spring, and now it's fall.

We're still here. I confess
we used to wonder whether we should go.
But the swung pendulum's advice was No,
never Yes.

At or up to the time indicated.
We're now past 2020, that Lost Year—
first in a series? Things still look dire.
What cancelled last year out has not abated,

but fulminates—the racking cough, the fever—
onward as far as anyone can see.
Is there a better place than this to be
constantly, still, continually, ever?

On our cold hill
the trees are bare.
Teach us to care and not to care.
Teach us to sit still.

In the Cloud

New York, December 2020

I made a list I can't find now
(where did all my folders go?)
of words my students didn't know.
Turmeric; poultice; fallacy;
cadence; meringue; Antigone;
Last but not least *Persephone*
are just a few that stick with me,
plucked from the poems that we read
(I tried to stay a week ahead)
between September and December.
Many more I don't remember.
But think of all the words they knew
or thought they knew. I thought so too.
Thinking too hard, though, doesn't do.
Words deeply pondered start to freeze—
as when before our tired eyes
Zoom stalls and stops (and no surprise),
leaving a dark screen, a blank hour
to fill with after and before.
Nonsense syllables devour
denotations. *Happy, sad;*
joyful or *lonely; good* or *bad:*
What does this mean to you? I said.
What does *beautiful* really mean?
I asked them as I tried to lean
into the noncommittal screen,
scanning until my eyes were sore
for the soul in each black square.
Were there really people there?
Did each name hide a secret face
sheltering somewhere in place,
some unimaginable space?
Each word they may have learned from me
in Gen. Ed. "Reading Poetry"

carries its meaning quietly
concealed behind the livid glow
of all we learned we didn't know.
Alone together, here we are,
stranded in our shared nowhere,
marooned in space, while, free from time,
meanings proliferate and chime
as words, unfettered, dance and rhyme.

Preexisting Conditions

New York, December 2020

Last summer in Vermont we made a labyrinth, to pace
and maskless breathe the sweet clean air and revel in the space.
Returning to the city, we were somewhat trepidatious.
From neighborhood to elevator, what would be contagious?
To walk on Broadway, it turns out, is labyrinth-pacing too:
we find a path and trace it, nod to people whom we know
or think we know by height, hair, hat, the color of their eyes.
Each day's like every other day and also a surprise.
It hasn't been so awful—more or less what we expected.
With masks and sanitizer we've felt more or less protected.
The final weeks of fall semester finished out on Zoom,
each of our students boxed into their separate little room.
Once school was over, we were free to focus on the reason
we'd come back to the city at this viral winter season:
to keep our endless medical appointments with a spread
of specialists so numerous they jostle in my head.
So what's the best taxonomy as I prepare to list
the whole brigade of doctors, making sure not one is missed?
By alphabet from Applebaum to Silverberg? Too dull.
Or anatomically from feet on upwards to the skull
with all those problematic teeth, defective, compromised—
crowns are in my future, and I'm not a bit surprised.
Or simply tick off body parts and ailments, each one's focus,
and classify each specialist according to their locus?
Here goes then. Ear/nose/throat man; oral surgeon; gynecologist;
and derma- cardio- ophthalmo- and gastroenterologist;
Two EKG's, one pelvic, one test of peripheral vision,
and scraping off a skin growth—now what else am I missing?
The years bring depredations much too tedious to mention.
But if I made a laundry list I'd start with hypertension,
then tack on osteopenia, ischemic colitis,
actinic keratosis—don't forget plantar fasciitis!
Lichen sclerosus too, and also hypercholesteremia,
and now the latest newcomer: add angioedema

(for these organ recitals it does help to know some Greek).
So what can I look forward to beginning in a week?
Implants and a mammogram await me. Time will fly
until the *pièce de résistance*: a colonoscopy.
Take a deep breath. I feel a bit beat up, but then remember
we've sloshed through this miasma from mid-March through
    December.
Welcome to the New Year. Somehow I've reached seventy-two,
and I have no idea how long I'll last. What about you?
This too shall pass—exactly how and when no one can tell.
And what we tend to overlook: we're passing on as well.
The pandemic reminds us we are prey to circumstance.
Meanwhile time isn't stopping. Years relentlessly advance.
Masked, facing forward, we can only try to look ahead,
balancing our mortal mix of hope and love and dread.

Blursday out of Breughel

New York, December 2020

Sooner than read another screed
about the societal costs of lockdown,
we walked out to the park and toward the river.

Focus. Performances. Spectatorship.
Children in brightly colored jackets
with sleds in neon colors and geometric shapes,
and adults too, whole families lining up
preparing to coast down the steep snow-slicked hill.
Winterscape out of Breughel:
everything sparkling, weather, respite, pleasure,
reminding me of what I can't remember.

That was Blursday. Thursday.
Today is Sunday, and the sky is grey.
The sun is hidden.
But the sunlight on the snow
was real, was there, we saw it:
low light angling through tall bare black trees
and a hawk on a naked branch
preening, posing, turning his little head,
showing us first one profile, then the other.
We spectators gathering for photo ops
ourselves attracted a secondary crowd.
People look up at people looking up
to see what they're looking at.
Societal cost of lockdown?
No. Just human nature.

The denizens of Breughel's world are preoccupied.
They go about their businesses and pleasures
taking at most a moment to notice one another.
To focus on one thing
is inevitably to ignore something else.

As if it weren't enough
mercy to live, or try to live, our lives
without paying attention to other people!
We have to pay attention.
We have to not pay attention.

In Auden's "Musée des Beaux Arts"
everyone in Breughel's "Icarus"
"turns away quite leisurely from the disaster":
the ship sails on, the ploughman goes on ploughing.
In Williams's "The Dance"
Breughel's swag-bellied heavy-footed dancers
sway to the squeal of bagpipes.
The poet reimagines and describes
and we the readers are doubly spectators.

Gathered spectators attract
what Canetti called an increase crowd.
The gazers at the hawk attract other gazers
until the hawk, bored, flaps and swoops away.
The Trojan elders gathered on the wall
look down at the battlefield. We watch them looking.
A knot of people in Riverside Park
move toward the group
standing near the wall gazing down
and at a careful distance
join that growing group.
What are they watching? Merely
brightly clad children lining up to slide
down a steep slick white hill
and clambering back up again,
small Sisyphuses, dragging their sleds behind them,
to take another turn.

That was Thursday. Today is Sunday.
The snow is dirty and melting.
The sun is hidden.
The longest night of the year is almost here.
But that day did happen.

We were there, we saw
the children in their snowsuits,
the families, talking, laughing through their masks,
pulling the sleds uphill, then up the stairs,
then across Riverside Drive and heading home.
Low sun through branches. Sky a little pink:
already almost sunset.

There was a smell like the river,
like ocean, like salt, like blood,
like spring—no, not yet.
Like—I remember now. The word is *hope*.

Grief Seminar

New York, January 2021

Those worlds we opened out to one another
have clung together and become one world.
And this merged world by now is so familiar
it has become transparent,
so hard to see it needs to be reimagined
like a stream that hides its source
and trickles underground.

Here on this island in a sea of danger
our created world is still familiar.
Even at the beginning
there was a fire burning on the water.
Even at the beginning
we weren't afraid to step through the red door.
Each of us held the key to a new kingdom.

Everything early in a love affair
is discoveries and omens,
fetishes, portents, symbols
of what at first we only guess at, yet
know we will not forget.
Later the meanings fasten themselves to story
and the story grows.

When I first dreamed about you
I held a printout in my hand, a roster
for a course called Grief Seminar.
You were one of the registered students.
Yours was in fact the only legible name on the roster.
The dream taught me that you were not immune,
somehow superior, to suffering.

But for each loss, each trouble added on,
there is a corresponding providential
erasure of a piece of the past,

so that we're never wholly overburdened.
We learn from what comes next.
What is behind us
we soon begin to mercifully forget.

Out the window in the early twilight
of the first week in January
(a sliver more light each afternoon),
I see masked promenaders strolling
along 101st Street toward Riverside Park.
When the time comes,
will we want to take off our masks?

The Cave

New York, February 2021

In C. S. Lewis's *The Silver Chair*,
Prince Rilian of Narnia, underground,
and the children sent to rescue him,
lulled and nearly vanquished by a spell
the lissome witch, the lamia, casts on them
(her sweet drugged powder smoldering on the fire,
insinuating strumming of her lute),
all but believe there is no realm above them,
no stars or moon, no rain or trees, no sky.
The cosmos is the cavern where they're gathered;
the underworld's in fact the only world.
Puddleglum's courage and the name of Aslan
release them to escape and see the sun,
but that's another story.
                                        So the cave
with its crowd of wan inhabitants,
prisoners habituated over time
to watching shadows caper on a wall—
we know it well. We've lived here for a year,
more or less. Time now is not the same.
And if and when we're free to leave this subterranean room
to venture up and out and smell the air,
some of us will prefer to stay inside
our cosy cave, as Socrates predicted.
It's hard to disagree. To face the light
would mean to take the measure of the changes,
gauge the extent of all the haunting losses;
to peer down empty vistas, finger relics,
open the doors of echoing auditoriums,
wonder about the purpose of such places:
who built them? Why? What were the builders thinking?
Many of us might swiftly scuttle back
into the burrow and adjust our chains,
focus again on what was interrupted—

the entertaining shadows on the wall.
"Strange prisoners," said Glaucon. "Like ourselves"
was the swift unanswerable reply.

I read this haunting fable years ago.
It floated back to mind the other day.
Having first checked the reference onscreen,
I padded down my cave's long winding hall
to the bookcase, found the book, the passage—
and there it was, and is. There it will be.
Patiently, patiently,
the allegory was waiting there for me.

The Ramparts

New York, February 2021

> *flammantia moenia mundi*
> —Lucretius, *De Rerum Natura*

Wait to be vaccinated.
Wait for spring to come.
Wait for the pandemic
to be over with and done.

Live in the present moment
is what the sages say.
But sliding sideways—future, past—
sometimes, suddenly:

isn't that what the mind does?
The after, the before:
we veer from our stale status quo
into their light and air,

twin vastnesses of memory
and of imagination.
How spacious it turns out to be,
our static situation!

And when at length we open
our doors and venture out
and look around and up and down,
will we then forget

the past year, masked and fearful?
The months will have flown by.
We'll see the running river.
We'll look up at the sky

and find our sense of who we are
may not be the same.

The world has walls, Lucretius wrote,
ramparts, all aflame.

That urgent cosmic vision,
beautiful, perilous—
may that be what we find we see
and may it stay with us.

In the Cold Courtyard

New York, February 2021

How sweet the strawberry at the edge of the cliff!
Through the cold courtyard snaked a waiting line.
I lectured about paradise—a myth.

Harsh spring sunlight glinted off a roof.
Slats of bright and dark drew a design.
How sweet the strawberry at the brink of the cliff.

All the flags were flying at half staff.
Transformations wrought by quarantine:
the list is long. Is paradise a myth?

It was—it is—too much. And not enough.
Days weeks months year: we have lost track of time.
How sweet the strawberry at the lip of the cliff.

Keep going. Days are lengthening. Love life
too much to understand or to explain.
What did I know of paradise—a myth,

an etymology, space cordoned off,
a tranquil haven, safe and soft and green?
How sweet the strawberry at the edge of the cliff.
I dreamed of teaching. Paradise: that myth.

The Second Shot

New York, February 2021

Vaccination lured us out of doors.
Approaching spring and the full moon
may also have helped draw everyone together.
But not too close. Not yet.
Through the cold courtyard, all around the block,
wound a line.
The wheelchair-bound, the leaners on their walkers,
these had priority—unwritten rule.
People were patient, even a bit cheery;
a spritz of subdued small talk.
One was no longer afraid, after a year,
to turn their masked face toward a stranger's face.
We couldn't wholly see each other;
we all could see the sky.

As you and I drove back from Canarsie—
the water out of sight but palpable
in the tremble and lambency of afternoon—
our hungry eyes were suddenly satiated
with a luxuriance of primary colors:
blood-red truck, yolk-yellow warehouse wall,
and two immensities, two shades of blue:
dark flowing river, overarching sky.

The Cave Again

New York, March 2021

Described by Plato, now it's much the same,
the underworld we're comfortable in.
Our fetters fit us like a second skin.
Enchanted by the caperings onscreen
and never by the hidden source of light,
the fire behind us or the naked sun,
we know each shadow perfectly by name.
Our children don't remember other ways.
We think we do; it's only been a year.
We think so, but the past's abstract and far,
ungraspable and tiny as a star
glimpsed from a distance of unnumbered days.

Up on the surface, dazzled by the glare,
squinting, stumbling, only gradually
able to make out moonlight, water, tree,
and gulping in the strange and strong fresh air,
how could some poor prisoners not rebel
if forced to leave their subterranean womb?
Would most not scuttle back to their dark room,
resist the power dragging them uphill?
Will we resurface—some of us, few, all?
The second spring approaches. Time will tell.

Tarot in Straus Park

New York, April 2021

The three of us were sitting on the stone
curved bench that afforded a rear view
of the statue and the fountain too,
with its inscription

In their deaths they were not divided.
Isidor and Ida drowned together.
We had arranged to meet (mild April weather)
with the friend who already had decided

on her solution to the one of many
riddles this year's been lavishly creating.
Yes, the virus seemed to be abating.
But was there any

assurance that it would be safe to go
to her niece's wedding, so long planned?
Each guest would be issued a colored armband
to signal social distance: yes or no?

Yes or no. How does one ever choose?
We offered, and she readily agreed,
divination. Did it meet a need?
Did she simply want to please

old friends? There was more to it than that.
She was a poet, and she yearned to know
answers life will not yield. Ask the Tarot!
So there she sat

between us, with a tea tray on her knees
to spread the cards on. Slowly, one by one,
she chose them; turned them over. Red blue green:
silent colors loud as a surprise.

Glances from a passerby or two.
Sparrows squabbled in a flowering tree.
What were we doing huddled there, we three?
Soft grey clouds with sunlight breaking through.

She'd told us that she wouldn't change her mind.
Flowery festivities, the south, the spring,
family obligation—everything
conspired to tighten all the ties that bind.

Time to go. My husband put away
the pack and with it what the cards had said
in their mysterious, venerable code.
I picked up the tea tray.

So what had we three seen?
A knight on horseback. Carpenters who fail
to raise a frame—the wands are all too frail.
A white-clad, star-crowned lady like a queen.

And this: blindfolded, a lone woman stands,
tightly bound and powerless to move,
her arms tied to her sides by—is it love?
She cannot even gesture with her hands.

She almost flaunts her immobility,
as if rigidity were a decision.
The fearful riddle's ominous solution
gives her permission to fly away,

drawn by the ties the cards so clearly show.
No space to reconsider, change her mind.
The marriage celebrations so long planned—
there never was a chance she wouldn't go.

Have a safe flight! Enjoy your time down there!
We parted at the corner. Now the day
was brightening. People strolled along Broadway,
doubly masked in hope and fear.

Too Soon to Tell

Vermont, July 2021

Looking around and taking stock,
a page from this new summer's almanac:
two cords of wood and more left over
should see us partway through next winter.
Last spring the low-grade fever: fear.
Too soon to tell about this year,
and it will always be too soon,
even now half this year is done.
When Odysseus reached home,
new trials, fresh variants, began.
Graceful sweep of soft green lawn
needing to be refreshed by rain.
Foxglove, primroses, and bee balm.
The gardener, leaning on her spade,
shook her head as she surveyed
the flowers: "Verticals! you need
more horizontals and more red."
Cot on the porch, patchwork bedspread:
I stretched out and tried to read
but lost the plot, drifted away,
gazing through pine boughs at the sky.
The book that dropped from my numb hand
taught something hard to understand:
Why People Die by Suicide,
which I'd forgotten having read
decades ago. But need again
now, because someone's in dire pain.
A person in the family's lost
his own life's plot—all joy and zest
precarious as that scraggly nest
on a low bough of the oak tree.
Squirrels in the attic—if not they,
who draped my green silk scarf that way,
wound it around a dangling wire

tightly enough to start a fire?
So much entangled; some things lost.
Lunch guests. Stuffed grape leaves. Make a list.
That memorial will be—when?
Give me the guests' names, says my son,
looking ahead to when I'm gone.
Death in a neighbor's family;
owl in another neighbor's tree;
the brook so low it's almost dry;
tomatoes plumping day by day.
Omen and vision, memory, dream,
spiderwebs jeweled in the cool dawn,
snake root, lupine, fairy ring,
currants already ripening.
Black raspberries are turning red.
I watch my love walk up the road,
soon or late to disappear
into the misty morning air.
Space is time here, Klingsor said.
"Let's choose up sides and go to bed,"
my drowsy mother used to say.
And then one more long summer day.
Mysterious bird's nest in the oak.
Words my long-dead mother spoke.

Afterword

The thirty-six poems here presented in chronological order were written between February 2020 and July 2021, a few in New York City but most in Vermont. Although they're not the only poems I wrote during those seventeen months, these particular poems cohere. All of them are touched by, and refer directly or indirectly to, the conditions imposed by the Covid pandemic—the many constraints and the sheer strangeness of that time; the unfamiliar ubiquity of dread. The selection begins on Leap Day 2020, a day which even then was tinged with an ominous proleptic weirdness, and closes in late July 2021, at a time when, however much we might long for closure or clarity, it's still, as the poem says, too soon to tell how events will further unfold.

These poems don't tell a story, precisely, but they do progress through time, and I came to think of them as a kind of almanac or journal. As they move through 2020 and halfway through 2021, the poems ride waves of emotion and experience; they constitute an almanac of moods as well as events—what Frost called inner and outer weather. Moods change constantly, of course, often, like weather in New England, many times a day; and the poems reflect some of these inner and outer changes. Still, the variety is probably less thematic than formal: a sonnet, a few villanelles, a poem in Sapphics, lots of rhymed tetrameter couplets. There's a love poem to my husband and a quasi-epistolary poem thanking a former student for her gift of vegetable seeds. One poem, "Preexisting Conditions," which catalogues the medical issues the quite healthy poet found herself listing, is so stuffed with polysyllabic medical terminology that it can (and probably should) be sung to the tune of Gilbert and Sullivan's "Modern Major-General." A couple of poems are dedicated to the friends who inspired them; another draws on the writings of my grandfather.

There's also a poem vowing not to teach on Zoom, and a poem written a few months later about teaching on Zoom. The latter poem includes the lines "Alone together, here we are,/stranded in our shared nowhere." These poems straddle that paradox. They're one poet's testimony to some of how it felt to live through this time, all the while aware that countless others were going through their own versions, their own challenges. We were alone; we were together.

The noisy horrors of the Trump presidency and the protests following George Floyd's murder make only fleeting and often indirect appearances here; the events of January 6, 2021, not at all. On these topics, others have already written, are presently writing, and will continue to write with eloquence and passion, and I trust we'll be reading and learning from their words for years to come. My own focus is private. But it's a shared kind of privacy. All of us, even the fortunate ones, among whom I certainly count myself, have been living through a time when the public and private can no longer be disentangled, if they ever could be. All of us, willy nilly, have been attending what one of the poems calls a grief seminar. We thought the seminar would have ended by now. It hasn't, but it keeps changing. And there are always more places at the table.

Poetry isn't a panacea, but its toughness and versatility and generosity have helped many of us. To write or to read a poem is to rediscover the amazing richness of the art I know I'm not alone in having come to love more than ever. The wealth and generosity of poetry have nothing to fear from the virus. Nevertheless, they're contagious. And how lucky we are that that's the case.

—Rachel Hadas
Danville, Vermont, August 2021

Acknowledgments

With thanks to the following periodicals, where some of these poems have appeared: *Literary Matters; Plume; Plough; Consequence; New England Review; Women's Review of Books; The New Yorker.*

"February 29, 2020" appears in the anthology *Stronger Than Fear*, edited by Carol Alexander and Stephen Massimilla (Cave Moon Press, 2022).

Heartfelt thanks to the family, friends, and students who throughout the strange months recorded here kept me company with their words and thoughts and even, occasionally, their physical presence. I don't want to make a list, for fear of leaving anybody out. I hope you all know who you are. A few of you are the dedicatees of poems in this pandemic almanac.

My beloved husband Shalom has been a sustaining presence day by day, hour by hour.

I am so grateful.

RACHEL HADAS is the author of numerous collections of poetry and essays, as well as a translator whose verse renderings of Euripides's two Iphigenia plays were published by Northwestern University Press in 2018. Her other recent books include *Love and Dread* and *Poems for Camilla* (both poetry), and *Piece by Piece* (essays). The recipient of honors including a Guggenheim Fellowship, the O. B. Hardison Award from the Folger Shakespeare Library, and a fellowship at the Cullman Center at the New York Public Library, Rachel Hadas is Board of Governors Professor of English at Rutgers University-Newark, where she has taught for many years.

www.ingramcontent.com/pod-product-compliance
Lightning Source LLC
Chambersburg PA
CBHW022001100426
42738CB00042B/1280